THE GOD OF INCREASE

How to Tap into God's Hidden Treasures

"Fear not, little flock; for it is your Father's good pleasure to give you the kingdom."
Luke 12:32 KJV

Dr. Anthony Walton

THE GOD OF INCREASE

Copyright © 2023 by Walton Publishing

All rights reserved.
No part of this book may be reproduced or transmitted in any form or by any means without written permission from the author.

ISBN: 978-1-7367209-3-6

Walton Publishing
Indianapolis, Indiana 46226

Printed in USA

DEDICATION

I dedicate this book to my family who have supported me in many of my endeavors. I also dedicate this book to those who have experienced hardships and have been able to persevere and overcome many difficult challenges and by the grace of God have been able to overcome them now becoming survivors.

I also dedicate this book to those in the church, as well as those outside of the church, who may have experienced personally or have been exposed to some type of mental health challenges. My prayer is that you may find and experience the Peace of God as you read through the chapters of this book.

Contents

Contents	iii
Introduction	1
Recognizing Our Purpose	3
Come Follow Me	6
God Speaks to Abram	7
God's Covenant of Circumcision	14
God's Promises for Sarah	15
Abraham's Response to God's Revelation	17
God The Creator	19
God Is Thinking of Us	21
Don't Give Up Until You Receive Your Increase	25
Caleb's Blessing Delayed but Not Denied	27
God's Principle of Investment	30
Operating In God's Timing	35
You Won't Believe Your Eyes	47
God's Increase	49
God Thinks of Us	51
Enlarge My Territory	53
More than Enough	56
Proving God for an Overflow	58
The Prophetic Blessing for The Shunammite Woman	60
Keep Your Eyes on God	63
Why Settle for Less	69
David's Judgement	73
Noah and the Flood	76
Commanded to Bear Fruit	79
Created to Bear Fruit	80
There Must Be Spiritual Growth	83
God Is My Source	86

Introduction

While reading this book, my hope is that you will come to know and understand to what extent God has made provisions for you and me to flourish receiving the best He has to offer. God desires for us to take full advantage of the unlimited resources He has made available for us to grow and become who, and what, He desires us to become. God wants to work through us, and in us, as we commit ourselves to Him.

It is further my desire that you realize how God wishes for you to experience tremendous increases in every area of your life. It is God's will for us to experience this great life changing increase, that will impact you positively while also affecting those who may meet you. As others witness and experience God's hand in your life, as you walk in the flow of God's Spirit and in obedience, developing an infectious spirit of optimism, faith, and belief; not only will they be impacted by you as they observe the God in your life, but their faith will be enhanced by your effective witness.

The God of Increase

"And I will establish my covenant with you, neither shall all flesh be cut off any more by the waters of a flood; neither shall there anymore be a flood to destroy the earth.

And God said, this is the token of the covenant which I make between me and you and every living creature that is with you, for perpetual generations:

I do set my bow in the cloud, and it shall be for a token of a covenant between me and the earth. And it shall come to pass, when I bring a cloud over the earth, that the bow shall be seen in the cloud:

And I will remember my covenant, which is between me and you and every living creature of all flesh; and the waters shall no more become a flood to destroy all flesh."

Genesis 9:11-15 KJV

Recognizing Our Purpose

We must be able to recognize our purpose and not give up on our dreams even when it appears they may seem to be out of our reach. If we are not able to identify our purpose, we will become disheartened finding ourselves falling short of the blessings God intends for us to have. No matter how difficult the challenges you must overcome may appear, just as long as you stay focused, stay on track, and keep your eyes on the vision God has given you, God will provide you with the provision. Even if all you have is a fish and two loaves of bread, hold on to that, or if all you have is one stone to fight off the giants in your life, just hold on to that stone and throw it with all you have within you, but whatever you do, don't give up no matter how long it takes to accomplish your goals, you must continue to believe in the power of God for your increase until you see it begin to manifest itself in your life.

Have you ever considered just how many promises God has promised us as believers? if we will only believe in Him and obey His commandments, we will begin to experience an enormous growth as well as His blessings in our lives. As we walk into our destiny of promises being fulfilled in us, we will become even bolder in our faith believing that God can and will do even more in us.

According to one account, there are approximately 3,573 promises in the Bible. The word Promise alone occurs over 50 times in the King James version. It should be obvious to you and me that it is the will of God for you to walk in His promise, purpose, and blessings.

In the next few pages, I will share with you some of what has been revealed to me regarding the blessings of God. I have received a revelation of what God has in store for you and me and how He desires for us to experience His abundant increase of blessings and not have need for anything.

The theme of being blessed is written throughout the pages of the entire Bible for those who will put their trust in God and obey his commands. This theme is either stated by using the words *Bless, Blessing* or *Blessed* or is written or implied within the scriptures. The words Bless, Blessings and Blessed are written in the Bible over 400 times.

The God of Increase

The word Blessed derives from the Greek term Makarios, which means "fortunate," "happy," "enlarged," or "lengthy." Makarios is used in the Septuagint (a translation of the Old Testament into the Greek language) and the New Testament to define the kind of happiness that comes from receiving favor from God. The idea behind makarios is that something is made "large" or "lengthy." When God "blesses" us, He "extends" His benefits to us. He "enlarges" His mercy on us. He "lengthens." He then will increase and multiply the blessings we already have into even greater blessings.

"O magnify the LORD with me and let us exalt his name together." Psalms 34:3 KJV

Come Follow Me

> *"Now the LORD had said unto Abram, Get thee out of thy country, and from thy kindred, and from thy father's house, unto a land that I will shew thee:*
> *And I will make of thee a great nation, and I will bless thee, and make thy name great; and thou shalt be a blessing:*
> *And I will bless them that bless thee and curse him that curseth thee: and in thee shall all families of the earth be blessed."*
> *So, Abram departed, as the LORD had spoken unto him; and Lot went with him: and Abram was seventy and five years old when he departed out of Haran"*
>
> *Genesis 12:1-4 KJV*

Abram who was comfortable in his homeland was given both a charge and a promise. He was told to leave both his kindred family and his homeland. Either of these requests would be difficult for the average person, but to be asked to do them both would take a strong conviction of one's faith in God.

God Speaks to Abram

God speaks a word to Abram. He tells him I have a request of you: I want you to let go of all you have, leave the country where you live, and go on a journey. I'm not going to tell you where I'm taking you right now, but I simply want you to have enough faith in my words to just trust, obey, and walk with me.

I cannot imagine what Abram was thinking of at that very moment. He might have been thinking "Look at all that I have to give up, all of this is too much to sacrifice?" When it comes to God, He sometimes causes us to experience a decrease before He allows us to experience His increase. I believe God does this so that when He ultimately blesses us, we will know beyond any shadow of a doubt that the blessings we have received are a direct result of what God has done for us and not of what we have achieved on our own works.

The God of Increase

> *"This is the LORD's doing; it is marvelous in our eyes."*
>
> Psalms 118:23 KJV

Sometimes we must give up what we view as valuable to receive from God that which is invaluable. Abram had no idea of the amazing journey that God was about to take him on. He had to make a choice not knowing that ultimately the choice that he would make would not only define his entire existence but for that of many generations to come.

Now let us look again at what God tells Abram. God at times will reiterate His promises to us to prevent us from becoming discouraged when we do not see the things we are expecting to receive from God as fast as we would like to see them. God's promises give us hope to hold on until we can see by faith, or in due process of time, with our natural eyes or are able to experience these blessings God has promised us for ourselves. God reiterates:

I will make of thee a great nation.

I will bless thee.

I will make thy name great.

I will bless you with such an abundance of blessings that you will be able to bless many others.

Abram, at this time, had no idea of the blessings that God was about to bestow on him as he would obey His voice and His directions.

Let's look again at what God promises Abram as well as how he responds as he listens intensely to what God is saying to him.

Blessings of Abram

Abram stepped out by faith being obedient to the will and purpose of God. God's request for Abram was accompanied by several promises.:

- God promises to increase his position and his prominence.
- God promises to make of him a great Nation.
- God promises to bless him.
- God promises to increase his seed at a time when he had no seed.
- God promises to make his name great.

The God of Increase

- God promises to bless him in a way that he would be able to be a blessing to others.
- God promises to be a blessing to those who bless you.
- God promises to curse those who would curse Abram.

God makes a Covenant with Abram

> *"And when Abram was ninety years old and nine, the LORD appeared to Abram, and said unto him, I am the Almighty God; walk before me, and be thou perfect.*
> *And I will make my covenant between me and thee and will multiply thee exceedingly.*
> *And Abram fell on his face: and God talked with him, saying,*
> *As for me, behold, my covenant is with thee, and thou shalt be a father of many nations."*
> *Genesis 17:1-3 KJV*

At a time when Abram felt the promise of God for him and his wife Sarai had slipped away and they would likely not be able to experience what God had promised them because they were beyond the normal age of being able to have a child, yet God speaks to him again and reiterates his promises to him.

God commands Abram to walk faithfully before Him in a perfect manner. Abram responds in awe by falling on his face in the presence of an almighty God who is now sharing with him His desire to multiply all that Abram possesses. I can only imagine the sense of astonishment Abram must have felt on hearing this.

God Changes Abram's Name to Abraham

> *Neither shall thy name any more be called Abram, but thy name shall be Abraham; for a father of many nations have I made thee."*
> *Genesis 17:5 KJV*

To show God's unconditional love and favor toward Abram, He now goes a step further bestowing a great impartation into Abram's life by changing his name from Abram to Abraham. In essence, giving him a new identity, thus solidifying his new identity with the great promises he had just received. I imagine this all had to be quite overwhelming to Abraham. But in the end, Abraham was true to obeying God's commands and continued to walk according to God's word in a perfect manner.

> *"As it is written, I have made thee a father of many nations,) before him whom he believed, even God, who quickeneth the dead, and calleth those things which be not as though they were.*
> *Who against hope believed in hope, that he might become the father of many nations, according to that which was spoken, So shall thy seed be.*
> *And being not weak in faith, he considered not his own body now dead, when he was about an hundred years old, neither yet the deadness of Sarah's womb:*
> *He staggered not at the promise of God through unbelief; but was strong in faith, giving glory to God;*
> *And being fully persuaded that, what he had promised, he was able also to perform.*
> *And therefore it was imputed to him for righteousness."*
>
> Romans 4:17-22 KJV

Abraham's Blessings Extended for Generations

> *"And I will make thee exceeding fruitful, and I will make nations of thee, and kings shall come out of thee.*
> *And I will establish my covenant between me and thee and thy seed after thee in their generations for*

The God of Increase

an everlasting covenant, to be a God unto thee, and to thy seed after thee.

And I will give unto thee, and to thy seed after thee, the land wherein thou art a stranger, all the land of Canaan, for an everlasting possession; and I will be their God."

Genesis 17:6-8 KJV

By one man's obedience, an entire nation was able to experience the blessings of God. These blessings that included an increase in the territory granted to him as well as to his children and his children's children throughout future generations.

God's Covenant of Circumcision

> *"This is my covenant, which ye shall keep, between me and you and thy seed after thee; Every man child among you shall be circumcised.*
>
> *And ye shall circumcise the flesh of your foreskin; and it shall be a token of the covenant betwixt me and you.*
>
> *And he that is eight days old shall be circumcised among you, every man child in your generations, he that is born in the house, or bought with money of any stranger, which is not of thy seed.*
>
> *He that is born in thy house, and he that is bought with thy money, must needs be circumcised: and my covenant shall be in your flesh for an everlasting covenant.*
>
> *And the uncircumcised man child whose flesh of his foreskin is not circumcised, that soul shall be cut off from his people; he hath broken my covenant."*
>
> Genesis 17:10-14 KJV

The covenant of circumcision involved the cutting away of the foreskin, this symbolizing the removing of the fleshly nature and allowing the spiritual man to take control. This covenant was a contract between Abraham and God and Abraham's descendants. This was to be a sign of their fidelity to commit to honoring God's word as God would honor His contract with them.

God's Promises for Sarah

> *"And I will bless her and give thee a son also of her: yea, I will bless her, and she shall be a mother of nations; kings of people shall be of her."*
> *Genesis 17:16 KJV*

God's promises given to Abraham were directed to Sarah, who was barren being childless in her old age. This is something that Abraham could not have imagined happening at this point in his and Sarah's life. Maybe it could have come to past fifty years ago, maybe even forty years ago but at this age in his life, it was well beyond what he could have ever had imagined for Sarah to be having her own biological child.

Sometimes we think the blessings that we desired for years have passed us by due to time and our physical limitations, but if God promises us something, time and or our own limitations will not hinder us from receiving what God has for us.

God speaks to Abraham and begins to promise him what he has always wanted but he did not understand the wonder working power of God to give him a biological son from Sarah who at this time was ninety-nine years of age, well beyond the age of childbearing.

God Changes Sarai's Name to Sarah

> *"And God said unto Abraham, as for Sarai thy wife, thou shalt not call her name Sarai, but Sarah shall her name be."*
>
> *Genesis 17:15 KJV*

Many times in the Bible we see where God changes a person's name. This is often done to symbolize the fact that he or she has gone from one level in God to an even higher level. It is often a sign of being empowered to perform a purpose God has preordained for that person to complete.

Abraham's Response to God's Revelation

Abraham laughs in response to God revealing to him His desire for him and Sarah to have a child, not through a surrogate, but their own biological child. Because this seemed so far removed from the ordinary, Abraham could but only laugh in amazement, wondering just how this could actually be happening.

> *"Then Abraham fell upon his face, and laughed, and said in his heart, Shall a child be born unto him that is an hundred years old? and shall Sarah, that is ninety years old, bear?*
> *And Abraham said unto God, O that Ishmael might live before thee!*
> *And God said, Sarah thy wife shall bear thee a son; indeed, and thou shalt call his name Isaac: and I will establish my covenant with him for an everlasting covenant, and with his seed after him."*
> *Genesis 17:17-19 KJV*

Whenever God chooses to increase our standing, our possessions, our position, or even our progeny, He can (and often will) defy the natural laws of man. Whenever God

The God of Increase

chooses to give you or me a supernatural increase, we must be willing to look far beyond what we are able to see with our eyes in the natural realm and be willing to look inward into the spiritual realm of endless impossibilities.

God The Creator

> *In the beginning, God created the heaven and the earth.*
> *And the earth was without form, and void; and darkness was upon the face of the deep. And the Spirit of God moved upon the face of the waters.*
> *And God said, let there be light: and there was light.*
> *Genesis 1:1-4 KJV*

We see here God can create something out of nothing. God speaks those things that are not just as if they had already come to the past.

Once we commit ourselves to putting our total trust and faith in God, we will then be able to unlock a treasure trove of blessings that God has afforded to those who will believe and trust in His miracle-working power. To be a recipient of God's precious promises, we must learn to apply the word of God to our personal everyday lives. Many believe God's words and promises when it comes to others but find it very hard, if not impossible at times, to apply these awesome promises and principles to their own circumstances.

The God of Increase

For me, it was always a challenge to believe that a great God who created the universe would think enough of me to pour out His bountiful blessings over my life. I often felt undeserving of the blessings I would receive, but as I learn to trust God more and more and learn to apply his word to my personal life, I began to flow in the intended blessings God had for my life. God not only did it for me but is willing to do it for anyone who is willing to place their trust in and act upon His word.

As I accepted and acted upon the word of God, I began to see so many blessings and miracles happen in my life that I could have never even imagined I would be able to experience.

As I acted upon God's word, I went from being a borrower to a lender. I went from robbing Peter to pay Paul to being able to have an abundance of resources, enough to be able to lend and to help others.

When we see the word of God in creation, He creates something from nothing. We feel we must have something to offer God for us to receive a blessing from Him, but that is not true, we do not have to have anything, but faith in His word.

THE GOD OF INCREASE

God Is Thinking of Us

> *"For I know the thoughts that I think toward you, saith the LORD, thoughts of peace, and not of evil, to give you an expected end."*
>
> Jeremiah 29:11 KJV

As I ponder over this verse, I see words of encouragement that transcends whatever I am going through. It tells me no matter what I am experiencing, I still have hope because I am assured that nothing happens to me that God does not allow. God has a plan for all His people who love Him and are obedient to His word. His thoughts are continually toward us even when we feel no one cares about us, we can be assured that God is thinking about us, even while we sleep.

> *"The steps of good men are directed by the Lord. He delights in each step they take."*
>
> Psalms 37:23 The Living Bible

This does not mean that everything we go through in life will be rosy, but we can have the assurance of knowing that whatever happens to us it must first be met with the approval of a God that loves and cares for us and desires to fulfill His purpose in our lives.

Countless scriptures verify God's desire to bless those who will believe in, trust in, and walk according to His word.

I would like to share with you a few scriptures that have been revealed to me that have impacted me to be able to be the beneficiary of an unlimited supply of God's heavenly resources.

Some of God's Promises

> *"For all the promises of God in him are yea, and in him Amen, unto the glory of God by us.*
> *Now he which established us with you in Christ, and hath anointed us, is God;*
> *Who hath also sealed us, and given the earnest of the Spirit in our hearts.*
> *Moreover I call God for a record upon my soul, that to spare you I came not as yet unto Corinth.*
> *Not for that we have dominion over your faith, but are helpers of your joy: for by faith ye stand."*
> *2 Corinthians 1:20 KJV*

The God of Increase

"Having therefore these promises, dearly beloved, let us cleanse ourselves from all filthiness of the flesh and spirit, perfecting holiness in the fear of God."
2 Corinthians 7:1 KJV

"Now to Abraham and his seed were the promises made. He saith not, And to seeds, as of many; but as of one, And to thy seed, which is Christ."
Galatians 3:16 KJV

"But, beloved, we are persuaded better things of you, and things that accompany salvation, though we thus speak.

For God is not unrighteous to forget your work and labour of love, which ye have shewed toward his name, in that ye have ministered to the saints, and do minister.

And we desire that every one of you do shew the same diligence to the full assurance of hope unto the end:

That ye be not slothful, but followers of them who through faith and patience inherit the promises."
Hebrews 6:9-12 KJV

"But now hath he obtained a more excellent ministry, by how much also he is the mediator of a better covenant, which was established upon better promises.
Hebrews 8:6 KJV

"By faith Abraham, when he was tried, offered up Isaac: and he that had received the promises offered up his only begotten son,"
Hebrews 11:17 KJV

The God of Increase

"Bring ye all the tithes into the storehouse, that there may be meat in mine house, and prove me now herewith, saith the LORD of hosts, if I will not open you the windows of heaven, and pour you out a blessing, that there shall not be room enough to receive it.

And I will rebuke the devourer for your sakes, and he shall not destroy the fruits of your ground; neither shall your vine cast her fruit before the time in the field, saith the LORD of hosts.

And all nations shall call you blessed: for ye shall be a delightsome land, saith the LORD of hosts."

Malachi 3:10-12   KJV

"Whereby are given unto us exceeding great and precious promises: that by these ye might be partakers of the divine nature, having escaped the corruption that is in the world through lust".

2 Peter 1:4 KJV

Don't Give Up Until You Receive Your Increase

We often find ourselves challenged when it comes to obtaining and walking into our full potential. For some, once they are faced with what appears to be an insurmountable obstacle to achieving their goals, they feel, because of their own self-doubt and fear of failure, that what they thought was for them really was not meant for them, so they are content to simply make excuses and just give up and quit, not receiving what God had in store for them all along.

God will allow doors of blessings to be opened in our lives. However, whenever the enemy sees you being blessed, he will allow someone, sometimes even those close to you, to try and discourage you, to block you from walking through the doors God has opened for you, to prevent you from just walking into your blessing. Don't let the enemy discourage you through doubt or unbelief, trying to close the doors. God has already given you the strength, the ability, the authority, and the power to open and walk right on into your blessings.

The God of Increase

> *"Because there is a wonderful opportunity for me to do some work here. But there are also many people who are against me."*
>
> 1 Corinthians 16:9 CEV

The old saying is "if at first you don't succeed, try, try again". This is so true. We cannot allow defeat in one area to define us and cause us to feel defeated in every area of our lives.

Take Your Mountain

There are times when God will simply drop a blessing down on your lap but there are other times when you must struggle to receive what God has for you. In other words, God is saying I will give you the tools and resources you need so you can receive your blessing, but you will have to take those tools and be willing to struggle and sometimes even fight against the forces of the enemy so you may be able to receive your blessings from God.

Caleb's Blessing Delayed but Not Denied

> *"And Moses sware on that day, saying, Surely the land whereon thy feet have trodden shall be thine inheritance, and thy children's for ever, because thou hast wholly followed the LORD my God.*
>
> *And now, behold, the LORD hath kept me alive, as he said, these forty and five years, even since the LORD spake this word unto Moses, while the children of Israel wandered in the wilderness: and now, lo, I am this day fourscore and five years old.*
>
> *As yet I am as strong this day as I was in the day that Moses sent me: as my strength was then, even so is my strength now, for war, both to go out, and to come in.*
>
> *Now therefore give me this mountain, whereof the LORD spake in that day; for thou heardest in that day how the Anakims were there, and that the cities were great and fenced: if so be the LORD will be with me, then I shall be able to drive them out, as the LORD said.*
>
> *And Joshua blessed him, and gave unto Caleb the son of Jephunneh Hebron for an inheritance."*
>
> Joshua 14:9-13 KJV

Here we see Caleb, a man of faith who trusted God and was fearless in the face of adversity, to the point when asked to spy out the land of Canaan and in the odds of those who lacked the faith to trust in the power of God to defeat their enemies, stood strong in his faith and believing that as long as God was with the people of Israel God would give them victory against all odds.

The God of Increase

Caleb had been promised an inheritance and even though it had been some forty-five years since he was given the promise and he was now about eighty-five years of age, he continued to believe in God for his inheritance. He chose to believe in God to give him the mountain that he desired all these years. God not only blessed him with an increased blessing of the land but blessed him to continue to maintain his strength for these many years from the time he first received the promise of an inheritance. His inheritance was not delayed because of lack of his faith, or desire to take it, but due to the lack of faith of those around him. But, because he did not let their lack of faith deter him, his blessings although delayed, were not denied.

> *"Trust in the LORD with all thine heart; And lean not unto thine own understanding. In all thy ways acknowledge him, And he shall direct thy paths."*
> *Proverbs 3:5-6 KJV*

The word of God reminds us we must always trust God for whatever we desire and not depend totally on what we see with our natural eyes or on how we feel things are going, but we must trust in God and seek His will for us in every situation.

The God of Increase

Sometimes the reason we are not able to accomplish a specific goal we have desired, may be because it may not be the will of God for us at that time, or maybe it is not God's will for us at all. But when we seek the will of God for our lives, He will direct us into an increased abundance of blessings designed especially for us as He guides us into His perfect will.

> *"For the vision is yet for an appointed time, but at the end it shall speak, and not lie: though it tarry, wait for it; because it will surely come, it will not tarry."*
>
> *Habakkuk 2:3 KJV*

Unfortunately, there are times when we get tired of waiting to receive an increase from God. Circumstances of life seem to be working against us, causing us to become frustrated and no longer trying to pursue what it was we were seeking . We must constantly be reminded of what God has promised you and me believing it will come to pass as we learn to wait patiently on Him.

> *"I waited patiently for the LORD; and he inclined unto me, and heard my cry."*
>
> *Psalms 40:1 KJV*

God's Principle of Investment
The Parable of the Bags of Gold

> *"Again, it will be like a man going on a journey, who called his servants and entrusted his wealth to them.*
> *To one he gave five bags of gold, to another two bags, and to another one bag, a each according to his ability. Then he went on his journey.*
> *The man who had received five bags of gold went at once and put his money to work and gained five bags more.*
> *So also, the one with two bags of gold gained two more.*
> *But the man who had received one bag went off, dug a hole in the ground, and hid his master's money."*
>
> Matthews 25: 14-18 NIV

This is a profound scripture in the Bible addressing personal responsibility and the ability for us to make individual wise and responsible common-sense decisions. As we examine this parable, we will come to understand the limitless abilities and gifts we have been given through the Holy Spirit. God gives us these gifts along with the free will to use our judgment to make wise choices. You and I must learn to grow and flourish wherever we are planted. In other words, regardless of what stage or state of life you are in, you can not only grow in that stage but can flourish as well.

We should never make excuses for what we lack but focus more on what we have and what it is that God desires to do in us, for us, with us, and through us, with what he has given us.

God equips you and me with all we need to survive, thrive, and increase in blessings and opportunities.

This scripture shows us that God never intends for us to be satisfied with anything less than our full potential and fulfillment of God's will and purpose in our lives. We should never be satisfied with just having enough but should always strive for more and more of what God desires for us to have. Note I did not say you should not be content but that you should not be satisfied.

> *"Not that I speak in regard to need, for I have learned in whatever state I am, to be content:"*
> *Philippians 4:11 KJV*

In these verses of scripture, the master was going on a journey and trusted each of his servants enough to give them a portion of his wealth. It appears his expectation was that they would make the most of the amount that was given to each of them. One was given five bags of gold, another two bags of gold, and yet to another a bag of gold. It is important to note that the man knew what each one was capable of being able to do with what he had been given. God will never give you and me more than what we are capable of handling. But God does expect us to make the best of what He has given us and not just sit on whatever He has given us. Whatever talent God gives us whether it be the gift of singing, preaching, teaching finances, construction works, encouragement, or support He expects us to use them to and for His glory and not allow the gifts to lay dormant and we not use them.

The one servant who was given five bags of gold was shrewd enough to increase his portion by doubling it to ten bags of gold. Likewise, the other servant who was given two bags of gold was also shrewd enough to increase the bags to four bags. The master recognized these two servants as being good and faithful. He could also recognize them as being faithful to what was given to them and doing their best to allow what was given them by their master to increase in value. However, the master was deeply disappointed in the servant who was given one bag of gold who did not have a

The God of Increase

vision, nor drive, and simply chose to dig a hole and bury of gold in the ground. Remember now that the master knew the ability of each servant who had received bags of gold from him.

The problem with the servant who buried his bag was that the master knew he could do much more with his bag than simply burying it. At the least, he could have put it in the bank, and it would have drawn some interest, but he essentially did nothing with it. That's why it is so important that we learn to maximize whatever gifts God gives us. God is a God of increase and expects and demands that we take advantage of whatever gifts He gives us, using them to His glory. This man is an example of a servant who had no ambition, nor foresight to do anything with what he had been blessed to receive other than to bury it in the ground.

Sometimes we want more from God and wonder why He does not give us all that we want, but the problem is we often take for granted what we have already been given and are not willing to use the gifts we already have. We should not expect God to give us more if we are not faithful with what we already have been given.

The God of Increase

This parable shows us that God expects us to use and grow whatever He has given us. God is not satisfied with our excuses of giving Him the bare minimum but desires us to give Him our very best and to take whatever He gives us and make the best of it. The master in the parable was, as God is with us, disappointed in the decision that was made by the servant who had the one bag and rather than commending him, he rather condemns him due to his complete lack of foresight in not utilizing what he had been given.

Operating In God's Timing

> *"And they gathered it every morning, every man according to his eating: and when the sun waxed hot, it melted. And it came to pass, that on the sixth day they gathered twice as much bread, two omers for one man: and all the rulers of the congregation came and told Moses."*
>
> *Exodus 16:21-22 KJV*

This scripture demonstrates to us that God knows what was needed and will at times give us just enough for what we will need to be sustained. He would give the children of Israel enough manna on each day to sustain them and their families but because they were to rest on the Sabbath, He gave them twice as much on the sixth day, and only on the sixth day did He give them enough for two days. This was a test of their faith in God that He would give them enough to sustain them. For those who lacked faith in God and tried to get more than what they needed it would began to stink and spoil. While God will at times give us what is needed for a specific time or purpose, He makes adjustments for what we need at any time and will provide us with increase to allow us to accomplish the task He has called us to perform.

> *"After this manner therefore pray ye: Our Father which art in heaven, Hallowed be thy name.*
> *Thy kingdom come, Thy will be done in earth, as it is in heaven. Give us this day our daily bread."*
> Matthew 6:9-11 KJV

For those who are content to make excuses for not being able to excel, I would encourage you from this day forward to not allow yourselves to make excuses for your failures in life. I know someone is saying "well you don't know my story". You're telling the truth, I don't know your story, but I do know your God.

Your story is less about you and more about your willingness to pursue the purpose of God in your life. In other words, you and I can begin to experience a reservoir of blessing as we began to reshape our mindsets. When we line up with the word of God, we will begin to experience an abundance of God's blessings.

THE GOD OF INCREASE

Let's look a little closer at the parable of the servants who were given bags of gold. There are several things I would like you to see:

FIRST

Just as the man was willing to entrust his wealth with his servant, so does God display a willingness to entrust His wealth, both naturally and spiritually with you and me.

> *"But we have this treasure in jars of clay to show that this all-surpassing power is from God and not from us."*
> *2 Corinthians 4:7 NIV*

What God has and is willing to do in our lives is to make available for us an abundance of His riches. God is willing to do for you and me what others cannot do, that is to take a clay vessel; (our bodies) which He already knows has many flaws, and we as well are aware of our many flaws, and yet God says to us "I know you are imperfect, but my love for you goes far beyond what you or anyone else can see with the naked eye, I can look beyond the cracks that are in you and perfect my love in you, and because of that I am willing to invest in you".

Whenever God invests in you or me, it is as if He is partnering with us. That means He does not just let us go at it alone but is willing to walk with us to lead and guide us into His perfect will while whispering into our ears the directions we need to accomplish His purpose.

> *"My sheep hear my voice, and I know them, and they follow me:"*
>
> John 10:27 KJV

SECOND

God gives you and me individual gifts based on our ability to receive them as well as what we are willing do with what he gives us. God knows before He gives us these gifts what our potential will be. Many of us will not operate in our full potential because we are afraid to use what God has given us.

THIRD

Faithfulness to whatever God entrusts with us is so important. We must be faithful to operate within the will of God with whatever He gives us. We must give due diligence to maintain a high standard of integrity and character.

THE GOD OF INCREASE

"His lord said unto him, Well done, thou good and faithful servant: thou hast been faithful over a few things, I will make thee ruler over many things: enter thou into the joy of thy Lord."
Matthews 25:21 KJV

FOURTH

The more God gives us the more He expects us to do with what He has given us. God expects us to do what we can with what we have.

"...For unto whomsoever much is given, of him shall be much required: and to whom men have committed much, of him they will ask the more."
Luke 12:48 KJV

FIFTH

Be fearless with what God has given you. Many of us have so many gifts and talents but what keeps us from operating in these gifts is fear of what others will think about us. You cannot allow fear to hinder you from operating in and using your gifts. You will never be successful if you are more concerned about what others think about you, rather than focusing on what God thinks about you and how to best utilize the gifts that God has given you.

The God of Increase

"When a man's ways please the LORD, he maketh even his enemies to be at peace with him."
Proverbs 16:7 KJV

SIXTH

When you fail to use what God has given you, you will often lose what has been given to you and watch as you see God giving it to someone else who will appreciate it more. I am reminded of the story of Esau and Jacob how that because Esau did not value his birthright, he was willing to exchange it with Jacob for a few morsels of food. Clearly it meant more to Jacob than it did to Esau. There are many people who would desire to have what you have, and you perhaps have taken for granted, not really realizing or appreciating the value of what you have.

SEVENTH

Finally, you must be willing to act upon what you have been given and mix it with faith for God to guide you into His purpose. In other words, there have been times when God has entrusted me with a gift, and I was not sure what to do with it. I wanted to prove myself worthy of the gift, so I took my insecurities to God in prayer. When I did this, God would reveal to me the direction I needed to take. We must learn to put our faith into action and then move forward on God's commands.

Earlier I mentioned how we often make excuses for our limitations or our lot in life. We make excuses such as, I was born poor, I was born with a particular handicap, I did not have the education of my peers, every time I try to do something this person or that person tries to hold me down, and the list goes on and on. I would encourage you, from this day forward, to quit making excuses for your shortcomings in life. Pick yourself up and begin to change your mindset. I know of many men and women who started from humble beginnings and through prayer, obedience to God, and continuing to believe in the power of God, were faithful in following the word of God and now have not only been able to grow but have been able to excel. There are certain principles that even non-believers have followed and have been able to gain the benefits of God's blessings.

The God of Increase

> *"That ye may be the children of your Father which is in heaven: for he maketh his sun to rise on the evil and on the good, and sendeth rain on the just and on the unjust."*
>
> Matthew 5:45 KJV

The man gave each person a bag, each bag had a specific value. It is not what God gives us but what you and I choose to do with what God gives us that really counts.

> *"And these are they which are sown on good ground; such as hear the word, and receive it, and bring forth fruit, some thirtyfold, some sixty, and some an hundred."*
>
> Mark 4:20 KJV

> *"O the depth of the riches both of the wisdom and knowledge of God! How unsearchable are his judgments, and his ways past finding out!"*
>
> Romans 11:33 KJV

It is amazing when we take into consideration the greatness of our God! When we consider His greatness in contrast to just how imperfect we are. As we think about this, it is mind boggling. It could easily cause us to feel insignificant as we view God from our own eyes. I sometimes ask myself, "What use would a great God like

The God of Increase

this have for someone flawed like me." I can relate to the prophet Isaiah when he saw a magnificent vision of the glory of God.

> *"In the year that King Uzziah died, I saw also the LORD sitting upon a throne, high and lifted, and his train filled the temple.*
> *Above it stood the seraphim: each one had six wings; with twain, he covered his face, and with twain, he covered his feet, and with twain, he did fly.*
> *And the posts of the door moved at the voice of him that cried, and the house was filled with smoke."*
> Isaiah 6:1-4 KJV

> He found himself utterly speechless at the grandeur and splendor of God. His only response was:

> *"Then said I, Woe is me! For I am undone; because I am a man of unclean lips, and I dwell in the midst of a people of unclean lips: for mine eyes have seen the King, the LORD of hosts"*
> Isaiah 6:5 KJV

> Many scriptures reveal to us our mindset is completely different from God's. We must not attempt to try and understand God from our limited understanding. Many of the things we received from God involve God revealing them to our spiritual man and not our carnal understanding.
> *"But the natural man receiveth not the things of the Spirit of God: for they are foolishness unto him:*

> neither can he know them, because they are spiritually discerned."
>
> 1 Corinthians 2:14 KJV

How we view ourselves and God's views of us are often completely different. Too often we are too critical of ourselves and at times not as critical as we should be, but God's assessment of us is never incorrect. Many scriptures confirm to us just how God views us and how his view is much broader than ours.

> "For my thoughts are not your thoughts, neither are your ways my ways, saith the LORD.
> For as the heavens are higher than the earth, so are my ways higher than your ways, and my thoughts than your thoughts."
>
> Isaiah 55:8-9 KJV

> "The LORD hath appeared of old unto me, saying, Yea, I have loved thee with an everlasting love: therefore with lovingkindness have I drawn thee."
>
> Jeremiah 31:3 KJV

> "What is man, that thou art mindful of him? and the son of man, that thou visitest him? For thou hast made him a little lower than the angels, and hast crowned him with glory and honour. Thou madest

> *him to have dominion over the works of thy hands; thou hast put all things under his feet:"*
> *Psalms 8:4-6 KJV*

> *"For God so loved the world that he gave his only begotten Son, that whosoever believeth in him should not perish, but have everlasting life."*
> *John 3:16 KJV*

These scriptures give us a panoramic view of the love of God for you and me. To become what God has designed for us to become, we must never lose sight of the value God has placed upon us, as well as how He sees us as His treasure.

The enemy comes in many ways to cause you and me to think and to feel we have little or no value, but I feel in my spirit to share with you right now, that if you only knew your worth in the eyes of God, you would not let another day go by without giving God a glorious Hallelujah praise, thanking Him not because we are worthy of his love and grace on our own , but God has extended His love and grace on us and counted us worthy who were unworthy. For this we should give God a glorious praise for what He has and is now doing in our lives on a daily basis.

The God of Increase

"I will praise thee; for I am fearfully and wonderfully made: marvellous are thy works; and that my soul knoweth right well."
Psalms 139:14 KJV

You Won't Believe Your Eyes

> *"But as it is written, Eye hath not seen, nor ear heard, neither have entered into the heart of man, the things which God hath prepared for them that love him."*
>
> 1 Corinthians 2:9

This scripture is a promise from God that even though we have seen many wonderful and splendorous things, the things we have already seen are in no comparison to what God is still preparing to reveal to us spiritually and naturally.

Some songs and sounds can move us to joy, tears, and laughter, and can even touch our souls, but I believe God has some sounds and words that we have not heard that will go far beyond what we have ever heard or seen.

God has just the word or sound that we need to hear to soothe our souls, comfort our hearts, and give us the strength to endure the challenges we must face in this life. As we draw closer to God, He will increase our ability to hear these secret sounds of the spirit and allow us to see what has often been hidden from us. As we continue to walk with

The God of Increase

God and begin to allow his spirit to lead and guide us, I believe God will take us into a realm of blessing that we will not be able to believe what our ears are hearing as well as what our eyes are showing us.

As we connect with God on a spiritual level, we will begin to see the intended increase of blessings God has prepared for us as we continue to abide in Him and continue to show our love for Him by being obedient to His will for our lives.

The God of Increase

God's Increase

"Now he that ministereth seed to the sower both minister bread for your food, and multiply your seed sown, and increase the fruits of your righteousness"
2 Corinthians 9:10 KJV

Let's look at this word increase. What do you think of when you hear this word? When examining the word increase, its meanings differ depending on how you look at it. I would like to visit this word as it has been revealed to me through the word of God. I am convinced that this word will take on a whole new and different meaning as you allow yourselves to explore it through the eyes of an all-loving, all-caring, all-knowing, all-powerful, and all-mighty God.

Increase:

• *Become or make greater in size, amount, intensity, or degree.*

• *grow, get bigger, get larger, enlarge, expand, swell; more.*

• *rise, climb, escalate, soar, surge, rocket, shoot up, spiral.*

The God of Increase

> • *intensify, strengthen, extend, heighten, stretch, spread, widen.*
>
> • *multiply, snowball, mushroom, proliferate, balloon, build-up, mount up, pile up, accrue, accumulate.*
>
> • *add to make larger, make bigger, augment, supplement, top-up, build-up, extend, raise, swell, inflate.*
>
> • *magnify, maximize, intensify, strengthen, heighten, amplify.*
>
> • *growth, rise, enlargement, expansion, extension, multiplication, elevation, inflation; more*

Throughout the scripture, it is revealed how God has a plan for us. Many times, we have fallen short of experiencing the blessings of God for lack of faith, due to fear, or hesitation in acting on God's word or just allowing the negative talk of others, our own negative self-talk, or the circumstances you see around you, to cause you to disbelieve what God has already promised you.

God Thinks of Us

When we quote Jeremiah 29:11; just how much attention do we really give to this scripture? Do we simply just gloss over its true meaning? or do we really understand what God wants us to hear and see when He states:

"For I know the thoughts that I think toward you, saith the LORD, thoughts of peace, and not of evil, to give you an expected end."

The question also is, do we really believe or have a true comprehension of what this verse is speaking to us as we reading through it?

We should be in awe as we come to understand how God is keenly aware of our every thought. God is aware of the desires of our hearts. He knows the inner thinking of what we desire and need. He knows our strengths, as well as our weaknesses, and yet He reminds us that His thoughts are constantly on us. His thoughts for us are not always of judgement and or punishment as the enemy would have us to believe, but rather of giving us peace, power, self-control, and a positive end that includes the increases of His blessings He expects us all to achieve.

The God of Increase

When we believe the word of God and stand on His divine promises, we will unlock a multitude of blessings that God has always intended for you and me to experience as we walk uprightly in his presence, trusting in His word to do for us just as He did for Abraham and his family. He can and will pour out unmeasurable blessings into our lives.

Enlarge My Territory

> *"Jabez was more honorable than his brothers. His mother had named him Jabez, saying, "I gave birth to him in pain." Jabez cried out to the God of Israel, "Oh, that you would bless me and enlarge my territory! Let your hand be with me, and keep me from harm so that I will be free from pain." And God granted his request."*
>
> Chronicles 4:9-10   NIV

The story of Jabez has always been a very fascinating story to me. It tells of a plain ordinary man having a genuine desire to increase what he had and not just be satisfied knowing that he served a God that could do exceedingly and abundantly above whatever he would think or ask of Him. Jabez was not satisfied by just hearing what God was able to do for him, but he also wanted to experience God's life changing ability for himself.

Jabez had every reason to throw his hands up in life and say a prosperous life must just not be meant for me to have. His mother in naming him was aware of the pain she experienced in giving birth to him and so named him to reflect the pain she experienced. No doubt every time his mother mentioned his name, she was reminded of the pain and hurt she experienced during his birth.

Jabez could have felt sorry for himself and just continued to make excuses for not achieving anything in life. He could have justified all the negative experiences that happened in his life and just chose to experience a negative fruitless existence based on the name he was given. If we allow ourselves to be defined by what others call us, or what they say about us, we will be blinded by their negativity or lack of understanding of our potential and purpose and fail to accomplish anything in life.

Rather than focusing on the pain and the negativity he and others around him had experienced, Jabez chose to trust in God and chose to have faith that God could and would turn his situation around. He petitioned God for better things and by petitioning God, began to experience an enormous blessing of increase enough to not only change the course of his life but also to change the course of others. When Jabez requested for God to increase and enlarge his territory he could not imagine just what all God would do for him.

Jabez requested four things from God:

THE GOD OF INCREASE

- To Bless Me
- Enlarge my territory.
- Let your hand be with me.
- Keep me from harm.

Somehow Jabez came into the revelation that God was a God of increase and as Jabez desired to do better and have more for himself, as well as his family, so was God willing to give him the desires of his heart. Because Jabez believed in God to grant his request God was gracious to grant his requests to him. When we have the faith to believe in God and trust in his promises, God will do for us as He did with Jabez and meet us right where we are.

"Ask and it will be given to you; seek and you will find; knock and the door will be opened to you."
Matthew 7:7 KJV

More than Enough

> *"And they spake unto Moses, saying, The people bring much more than enough for the service of the work, which the LORD commanded to make. And Moses gave commandment, and they caused it to be proclaimed throughout the camp, saying, Let neither man nor woman make any more work for the offering of the sanctuary. So the people were restrained from bringing. For the stuff they had was sufficient for all the work to make it, and too much"*
> *Exodus 36:5-7 KJV*

Whenever the body of Christ decides to work together in unison, we will lack for nothing. While they were building the Tabernacle as a place of worship that God had given them the design to build, God gave the men gifts of workmanship and wisdom and others gifts of understanding needed to perform the various works to be used in for building of the Tabernacle to make the vision come to pass.

Moses also requested those whose hearts would make them willing to freely give an offering toward the building and supplying of the Tabernacle to support through their giving. In a display of faith and unity, because of the love of God and the desire to furnish the Tabernacle the

The God of Increase

people brought so much that Moses had to tell them to stop bringing gifts. I often wonder what would happen if the people of God were able to display this type of faith and unity today. I imagine the possibilities would be endless.

When we choose to obey the voice of God and act in love unselfishly, God will give us such an increase that it will amaze us.

It is God's desire to increase whatever he gives us to do and to allow it to expand beyond our imaginations. The people were of one accord and allowing themselves to receive an abundance of God's blessings. Whenever you, your church, your family, your business, or your community decide to work together you will receive an abundance of God's blessings.

Proving God for an Overflow

> *"Bring ye all the tithes into the storehouse, that there may be meat in mine house, and prove me now herewith, saith the LORD of hosts, if I will not open you the windows of heaven, and pour you out a blessing, that there shall not be room enough to receive it."*
>
> *Malachi 3:10 NLT*

Here God gives a command followed by a conditional blessing. He simply tells them to bring into the house of God a tenth of their increase as well as an offering, and He would give them such an increased amount of blessing above and beyond what they had given to Him, that there would not be enough room to receive what God was going to do in return for their sacrifice.

God reminded them of their obligation to support the house of God but also in turn tells them by being obedient to His word he would multiply back to them that which they had given.

When we choose to prove God or rather to test His spiritual theories, we will be guaranteed to receive the

The God of Increase

blessings that God has promised us in being obedient to His word. We must not be afraid to prove or stand on God's word, but always stay before His presence having an expectation of Him fulfilling His promises to us.

I encourage you to begin to speak to God regarding the things that are near and dear to your heart and not be afraid to step out on His word in faith, believing He will do what his word says He will do.

The Prophetic Blessing for The Shunammite Woman

"And it happened one day that he came there, and he turned in to the upper room and lay down there. Then he said to Gehazi his servant, "Call this Shunammite woman." When he had called her, she stood before him.

And he said to him, "Say now to her, 'Look, you have been concerned for us with all this care. What can I do for you? Do you want me to speak on your behalf to the king or to the commander of the army?'"

She answered, "I dwell among my own people." 4 So he said, "What then is to be done for her?"

And Gehazi answered, "Actually, she has no son, and her husband is old."

So he said, "Call her." When he had called her, she stood in the doorway. 16 Then he said, "About this time next year you shall embrace a son."

And she said, "No, my lord. Man of God, do not lie to your maidservant!"

2 Kings 4:11-16 NKJV

THE GOD OF INCREASE

The story of the Shunammite Woman A Story of God's Reward for Our Deeds

> *"But, beloved, we are persuaded better things of you, and things that accompany salvation, though we thus speak.*
> *For God is not unrighteous to forget your work and labour of love, which ye have shewed toward his name, in that ye have ministered to the saints, and do minister"*
>
> *Hebrews 6:9-10 KJV*

The Shunammite Woman was a wealthy woman who lived on the main road through Shunum. She was married to an older man, and they had no children. This woman had the heart of a servant and had a desire to unselfishly and graciously be a blessing to the man of God as he would travel through her land, so much to the point that she reserved a special place on her property for him to rest and be fed any time he would come through Shunum.

On one visit, the man of God being discerning, knew something was missing in her life and even though she never complained or expressed the emptiness she felt of not having a child, the prophet was able, by the spirit of God, to discern her hurt, and having compassion for her pain, spoke a word of blessing to her.

Even though what the Shunammite woman had done for the man of God was purely out of respect for his position and her not requesting or wanting anything from him, he was able to discern that something was missing from her life. He then spoke a prophetic word into her life of her being blessed by the next year to have a child. The woman was married to a man that was older than she and probably physically unable to give her a child. But the word of God will supersede what our natural limitations and circumstances are.

The Shunammite woman, by having a servant's heart, was rewarded by a supernatural act of God according to the prophecy the man of God had given her, within a year, she was blessed to have had the experience of an increase from God in the form of gift of the having a precious and welcomed son.

The God of Increase

Keep Your Eyes on God

In the times in which we are living , many people are concerned about their future. We are frequently preoccupied by so many things that can catch our attention causing us to become easily distracted, fearful of moving forward, afraid to let go of what we have in order to receive what God has for our future.

The good news for the believer is that not only do you not have to worry about holding on to what you have, but as you place your trust in God, He will allow you to see and experience an abundance of blessings and an increase of even more than what you currently have.

> *"But as it is written, Eye hath not seen, nor ear heard, neither have entered into the heart of man, the things which God hath prepared for them that love him."*
> *1 Corinthians 2:9 KJV*

Some would have you to think God does not want you to be blessed. It's like the enemy wanting you to think you must beg God for what you want from Him or whatever you would like for God to do in your life. But the truth of the matter is, as the Scriptures admonish us.

> *"Fear not, little flock; for it is your Father's good pleasure to give you the kingdom."*
> *Luke 12:32 KJV*

You do not have to beg God for anything. We must continue to have faith in God to do the impossible for us.

> *"Be careful for nothing; but in everything by prayer and supplication with thanksgiving let your requests be made known unto God.*
> *And the peace of God, which passeth all understanding, shall keep your hearts and minds through Christ Jesus."*
> *Proverbs 3:5-6 KJV*

Many of the scriptures we read tell us about the love of God and His desire to give us the desires of our hearts. The following are a few scriptures that have been a blessing to me throughout the years.

> *"Delight thyself also in the LORD: and he shall give thee the desires of thine heart."*
> *Psalms 37:3-4 KJV*

This same scripture in the amplified Bible states it this way:

> *"Trust [rely on and have confidence] in the LORD and do good; Dwell in the land and feed [securely] on His faithfulness.*
> *"He will give you the desires and secret petitions of your heart."*
>
> Psalms 37:3-4 AMP

There are things we want from God that if we were to share with others it would seem so farfetched from our reality that it would make them laugh if you were to share it with them. These are the things the scripture refers to when it talks about and speaks on the secret petitions of our hearts.

We all have dreamed of things we would like to see or experience. However, whenever we become frustrated with our circumstances and fail to dream, we lose hope for a better position in life. If I am to receive anything from God, I must have the faith to believe in Him and trust that God will do what He has promised even if what I want from Him is so removed from where I am that it will make me (and others) laugh about it.

The God of Increase

> *"And the LORD said unto Abraham, Wherefore did Sarah laugh, saying, Shall I of a surety bear a child, which am old?"*
>
> *Genesis 18:13 KJV*

I am convinced more than ever that God is preparing us to walk in a season of blessings where we can begin to ask God for things that we once thought to be well out of our reach and beyond our wildest imagination. That does not mean that everything is going to be perfect, but I do believe, according to the word of God, the only thing holding us back is faith in God for the impossible. Look at where you are, For many of us we have accomplished far more than our forefathers were able to imagine for us or even what we could have imagined years ago for ourselves. Even if you are not where you ultimately want to be. If you look at your current situation and it feels as though you are worse off than you were in past years, I encourage you to keep on believing and trusting in God for a better future. Your increase is on the way!

> *"He said, "Daniel, you who are highly esteemed, consider carefully the words I am about to speak to you, and stand up, for I have now been sent to you." And when he said this to me, I stood up trembling.*
> *Then he continued, "Do not be afraid, Daniel. Since the first day that you set your mind to gain*

understanding and to humble yourself before your God, your words were heard, and I have come in response to them.

But the prince of the Persian kingdom resisted me twenty-one days. Then Michael, one of the chief princes, came to help me, because I was detained there with the king of Persia."
Daniel 10:11-13   NIV

"And the children of Israel said unto them, Would to God we had died by the hand of the LORD in the land of Egypt, when we sat by the flesh pots, and when we did eat bread to the full; for ye have brought us forth into this wilderness, to kill this whole assembly with hunger."
Exodus 16:3 KJV

The children of Israel because of what they were perceiving to be a desperate situation they were in while in Egypt, rather than believing and trusting in the plan of God, began to lose hope and desired to be in bondage, actually willing to accept a life of serving Pharaoh (which, because of the challenges set before them) appeared to be a better choice! This seemed to be a better choice for them because of their unbelief. For a period, rather than trusting in God and having an opportunity of enjoying the privileges of freedom God had intended for them to have, they became stuck in unbelief, falling short of receiving the promises of

God for their future, due to their unbelief. Because of their unbelief they were in the wilderness some forty years when they could have been experiencing the blessings of God instead.

Your situation might look hopeless but if you can believe in God, I am convinced that God, amid whatever challenges you might be facing is allowing you to experience the shaping of your miracle. We are too quick to settle for less, rather than to believe God for the best. We can be our own worst enemies. Had not the children of Israel had their wilderness experience, there would not have been a promised land in their future. We must be willing to accept our wilderness experiences but at the same time be willing to trust in God for our promised land.

> *"But without faith it is impossible to please him: for him that cometh to God must believe that he is, and that he is a rewarder of them that diligently seek him."*
> *Hebrews 11:6 KJV*

The only limitation we have is our lack of faith. Are you willing to take God at His word? Are you willing to believe in God's best for your life?

Why Settle for Less

References of Increase is mentioned in the Bible over one hundred and fifty times. This is a powerful word and when it comes to receiving a positive and powerful increase creates a sense of feeling uplifted and hopeful for the future for the believer as he or she puts their trust in God for more of what he or she is experiencing.

Increase:

An instance of growing or making greater:

Become or make greater in size, amount, intensity, or degree.

I remember as a young man in elementary school, I had a teacher that encouraged the class to be the best they could be. As an incentive, he told the class that he would take them to whatever restaurant they chose to go to if they made an "A" on a grammar project. I had never gotten an "A" in my life prior to this but because of the offer, I found myself studying harder than I had ever done before. When I got my grade back, to my amazement, I was surprised to see that I had received an" A" for the first time in this class. We must be willing to push ourselves and make sacrifices to experience God's increase in our lives. Just as I was willing to push myself and make sacrifices to get an "A" we must be willing to push and make sacrifices to receive the things of God.

My professor said he was not surprised to see that I had gotten an "A". What he realized was that I was performing at a level far less than what he saw me as being capable of doing. I previously had chosen to not be my best, not increase my ability and output, but to just settle for anything. Because of my performance, the teacher said whatever restaurant I wanted to go to he would pay for it. I thought about it for a while and decided that I would choose Burger Chief, (which is now called Burger King). Now I could have gone to any restaurant of my choosing, but of all my choices, I ended up choosing a simple restaurant. Many times, we settle for far less than what God wants to provide for us.

The God of Increase

Receiving an increase in the things of God is not simply an option but should be an expectation of those who desire to experience the fullness of what God wants for you and me.

"Why be jealous of others when all you have to do is ask your heavenly Father for what you want" ~ AW

> "You are jealous and covet [what others have] and your lust goes unfulfilled; so you murder. You are envious and cannot obtain [the object of your envy]; so you fight and battle. You do not have because you do not ask [it of God].
> You ask [God for something] and do not receive it, because you ask with wrong motives [out of selfishness or with an unrighteous agenda], so that [when you get what you want] you may spend it on your [hedonistic] desires."
>
> James 4:2-3 AMP

One sad story in the Bible tells us of how King David failed to understand and believe how God was all that he needed.

Before David had been confronted by Nathan, the prophet, he was caught up in a situation where he could not see beyond his own selfish desires. Rather than allow God to provide for him with what was meant for him, he chose to commit adultery and later murder to cover up his deed all to satisfy his own lustful and selfish desires.

Nathan revealed to King David that God was willing to go to great lengths to show David just how great he could and was willing to be in his life. We often settle for less when God wants to give us so much more than what we want for ourselves.

> "I also gave you your master's house and put your master's wives into your [a]care and under your protection, and I gave you the house (royal dynasty) of Israel and of Judah; and if that had been too little, I would have given you much more!"
> 2 Samuel 12:8 AMP

David's Judgement

The prophet Nathan shared with King David the story of a poor man who only had one ewe lamb and how that one lamb was taken from him by the rich man who had many.

Before the prophet disclosed to King David the true meaning of the story and his purpose for sharing the story, King David was immediately angered by what he had heard. However what David was not aware of was Nathan's reason for sharing the parable. It was because he had come to rebuke and expose David for his sin. David was incensed and immediately pronounced judgment on the other person until it was revealed to him that the prophet was really speaking of David's action in desiring another man's wife so much that he had committed adultery with her and later went as far as to place her husband in a position to be killed so he could have her for himself as well as attempting to cover up his sin.

What God has for you it is for you. God revealed to David that His love for him was so great that he would have been willing to afford to David unlimited blessings, and all David would have had to do was to simply ask God. But instead, King David allowed his own lust and desire to rob

THE GOD OF INCREASE

him of many of the blessings God would have given him if he had only made his petition to God for them. Because of this not only did King David miss out on many of the blessings God would have been willing to extend to him, but he also suffers many challenges within his own home as a result of yielding to his flesh. His actions prevented him from being able to build a temple for God.

I am glad to know that when I pray to a loving God and humbly submit myself to his will, I can be confident in knowing that He will grant me the things I desire of Him as I seek His divine will for my life.

> *"But seek first his kingdom and his righteousness, and all these things will be given to you as well."*
> *Matthew 6:33 NIV*

If you desire a blessing from God and are willing to stretch out on God (take God at his word) believing for the impossible for you and those around, you will experience God's increase in your life as you walk in faith and continue to believe in the power of God.

This story should remind us of how we can become misguided when we are led away of our own lust and desire can easily missing the will of God for our life. There are many things God has for us, but we must first position ourselves in His presence to hear and know His will in order to receive God's great blessing that will grow exponentially as our faith increases and as our desire to experience God's supernatural overflow.

Many people want to receive supernatural increases from God but are unwilling to allow themselves to be led by the Holy Spirit. For God to increase in our spiritual lives the flesh must decrease. We must stay focused on the things of God and not allow ourselves to become distracted by the things of the world which will ultimately perish.

> *"For whosoever will save his life shall lose it; but whosoever shall lose his life for my sake and the gospel's, the same shall save it.*
> *For what shall it profit a man, if he shall gain the whole world, and lose his own soul?*
> *Or what shall a man give in exchange for his soul?"*
> *Mark 8:35-37 KJV*

Noah and the Flood

"And God spake unto Noah, and to his sons with him, saying,
And I, behold, I establish my covenant with you, and with your seed after you;
And with every living creature that is with you, of the fowl, of the cattle, and of every beast of the earth with you; from all that go out of the ark, to every beast of the earth.
And I will establish my covenant with you, neither shall all flesh be cut off any more by the waters of a flood; neither shall there anymore be a flood to destroy the earth.
And God said, This is the token of the covenant which I make between me and you and every living creature that is with you, for perpetual generations:
I do set my bow in the cloud, and it shall be for a token of a covenant between me and the earth.
And it shall come to pass, when I bring a cloud over the earth, that the bow shall be seen in the cloud:
And I will remember my covenant, which is between me and you and every living creature of all flesh; and the waters shall no more become a flood to destroy all flesh.
And the bow shall be in the cloud; and I will look upon it, that I may remember the everlasting covenant between God and every living creature of all flesh that is upon the earth."

The story of Noah and his family being delivered by God through the protective covering of the ark is a remarkable story displaying God's judgment tempered with his mercy covered by his love and his promise to us of a brighter tomorrow.

The Word of God displays a vast array of God's judgments, miracles, grace, forgiveness, and love. In all of, this God gives us hope for a better tomorrow.

Noah Finds Grace

> *"And it repented the LORD that he had made man on the earth, and it grieved him at his heart.*
> *And the LORD said, I will destroy man whom I have created from the face of the earth; both man, and beast, and the creeping thing, and the fowls of the air; for it repenteth me that I have made them.*
> *But Noah found grace in the eyes of the LORD."*
> *Genesis 6:6-8 KJV*

The Bible tells us that even though there was evil all around Noah that he was able to find favor in the sight of God.

As we examine the word of God, we see revealed to us a rich trove of God's love for us and His desire to supply us with an abundance.

Noah was able to draw close enough to God, regardless of what others around him were doing. The Scriptures tell us that Noah found grace in the eyes of God. The times in which Noah lived in (just as today) were turbulent times, and Noah had to make a choice to follow God or to go along with what was popular and what was the trend of his times.

Regardless of what is going on around you, you can experience the grace of God as you walk in the spirit and allow God's spirit to lead and guide you. Now when we look at this story, God pronounces judgment on the land but because Noah had found favor in the eyes of God, not only was he spared from losing his life in the flood, but his entire family was also spared.

Commanded to Bear Fruit

"And you, be ye fruitful, and multiply; bring forth abundantly in the earth, and multiply therein."
Genesis 9:7 KJV

Because God had destroyed all living creatures on the earth, Noah and his family were commanded to be fruitful and to multiply. For life and civilization to continue, there had to be a repopulation of the entire earth. It was the responsibility of Noah and his family to make this happen. Had they not done this there would have no longer been a continuation of growth on the earth.

As with Noah, we are commanded to be fruitful when it comes to the work of the ministry. We should not be satisfied in our local churches praising God and singing to each other but after we finish our corporate worship in our local church, we should commit ourselves to staying focused on the work of the Lord by ministering to others and bringing them into the kingdom to experience the wonderful working power of God to change their lives.

Created to Bear Fruit

> *"He spake also this parable; A certain man had a fig tree planted in his vineyard; and he came and sought fruit thereon, and found none.*
>
> *Then said he unto the dresser of his vineyard, Behold, these three years I come seeking fruit on this fig tree, and find none: cut it down; why cumbereth it the ground?*
>
> *And he answering said unto him, Lord, let it alone this year also, till I shall dig about it, and dung it:*
>
> *And if it bear fruit, well: and if not, then after that thou shalt cut it down."*
>
> *Luke 13:3-6-9 KJV*

This story demonstrates to us that every living creature upon the face of the earth has a purpose.

We all have a purpose we are to fulfill if we are to become what God expects of us.

We as Christians must understand our purpose as it pertains to God. If you are not aware of your purpose, I encourage you to pray and ask God to reveal His purpose to you.

The God of Increase

Whenever we fail to realize our purpose, we are like the tree that should have borne fruit but did not. It looked good to the eye, it had the potential to bear fruit which was what its purpose was but unfortunately, it bore no fruit. As with the fig tree so are we when we fail to operate in our purpose, God becomes dissatisfied with what we are doing. Because of God's mercies and grace, He will many times give you and me an opportunity to allow ourselves to become fruitful by walking in our divine purpose and if not may and often will pronounce judgement over us.

The choice is up to us whether we are willing to allow ourselves to experience an increase from God or chose to reject God's opportunity for us to receive an unlimited amount of blessings. I believe we have a mandate from God not only to just survive but to thrive as we operate in our full potential.

As with the fig tree, God does not immediately give up on us but allows us time to produce purpose in our lives. He will sometimes send people into your life to help cultivate you and to allow you to increase in whatever ability or talent God has given you. Unfortunately for those who will not allow themselves to experience the increased blessings of God, they will very well be like the fig tree that Jesus cursed because it was not producing anything. Don't focus merely on looking good but focus on doing good and producing your harvest.

We serve a great God that is a God of blessing and demonstrates His love toward us by allowing and affording us the opportunity to experience His increase in everything we do.

God desires for you and me to experience an abundance of His increase. To please Him, we must recognize that God is concerned about seeing increases in our lives. We should be better and do better today than we did yesterday, and we should be willing to be, and do even better tomorrow than we were today to experience God's great increase in our lives.

From this day forward, my prayer is that you come to see God as a God of increase and began to walk in and to expect to experience the blessings of God as you put your trust in Him.

There Must Be Spiritual Growth

> *"According as his divine power hath given unto us all things that pertain unto life and godliness, through the knowledge of him that hath called us to glory and virtue:*
> *Whereby are given unto us exceeding great and precious promises: that by these ye might be partakers of the divine nature, having escaped the corruption that is in the world through lust.*
> *And beside this, giving all diligence, add to your faith virtue; and to virtue knowledge;*
> *And to knowledge temperance; and to temperance patience; and to patience godliness;*
> *And to godliness brotherly kindness; and to brotherly kindness charity."*
> 2 Peter 1:5-7 KJV

In our walk with Christ there must be spiritual growth if we are to fulfill our God given purpose. Just as in the life of a newborn infant it is expected for the child to have a normal growth pattern. If at any point the child is no longer growing, there would be a problem. For the child to grow and become strong, the child must go through a strong developmental process for there to be healthy growth.

Just as in the natural development, if a man or woman of God are to be used of God and experience God's spiritual growth there must be a healthy spiritual maturity in their life causing them to build a godly lifestyle.

For every child of God, as has been stated earlier, God has equipped him or her with the tools, they need to be the best version of themselves they can be in order to become what God has designed for him or her to become.

> *"According as his divine power hath given unto us all things that pertain unto life and godliness, through the knowledge of him that hath called us to glory and virtue:"*
> 2 Peter 1:3 KJV

Now let's take a closer look at verse by verse of the Scriptures we have just read:

This verse is a reminder to the believers that God has empowered us with his divine power and is allowing us unlimited access to all things that pertain unto life and godliness. With this knowledge in mind, I can boldly proclaim who I am in God and what God has enabled me to do and become.

God Is My Source

> "....., through the knowledge of him that hath called us to glory and virtue:"
> 2 Peter 1:4 KJV

Peter shares with us what God has given us, but I think it is equally important as Peter shares with us, just how we are able to obtain this increase. He states it is through the knowledge of God. When we have a knowledge of what God can do for us, we are then required to tap into the source of our blessings which is knowing as much as we can about God and His plans for us as we can.

> "Take my yoke upon you and learn of me; for I am meek and lowly in heart: and ye shall find rest unto your souls."
> Matthew 11:29 KJV

When we can recognize the source of our blessings, we then are able to know where to go and how to tap into that source whenever we have a need, being confident, we are going to the right source who is able to supply all of our needs.

The God of Increase

> *"But my God shall supply all your need according to his riches in glory by Christ Jesus."*
> *Philippians 4:19 KJV*

Peter lays the foundation for the believer to be able to access the blessing of God and receive a number of increased blessings when he or she begins to add to what they already have.

Faith is the key to receiving anything from God so it should be of no surprise that Peters starts off with faith as being the foundation on which he builds these verses on.

> *"And beside this, giving all diligence, add to your faith virtue; and to virtue knowledge;" 2 Peter 1:5 KJV*

> *"But without faith it is impossible to please him: for he that cometh to God must believe that he is, and that he is a rewarder of them that diligently seek him"*
> *Hebrews 11:6 KJV*

As we seek to please God and receiving our Increases into the promises of God, we must begin with faith, an unshakable believe in the word of God that God will do just what he says he will do.

THE GOD OF INCREASE

Strong's definition of virtue implies moral goodness. What good will it do for a person to have faith to move mountains and not display a simple characteristic of displaying the act of moral goodness in their life. Without virtue everything you do will become defiled by your carnal actions.

As a person increases in the things, they receive from God it should bring about a forward moving progression of change in their life and not a moral or backwards decline.

Again, here we see the importance of having a knowledge of the will and plan of God. This will allow you to stay in sync with God. As we grow in the knowledge of God, we will be able to have a better understanding of what is required of us.

"Wisdom is the principal thing; therefore, get wisdom: and with all thy getting get understanding."
Proverbs 4:7 KJV

"And to knowledge temperance; and to temperance patience; and to patience godliness;"
2 Peter 1:6

The God of Increase

After we have obtained knowledge of God we must not get puffed up with pride or arrogance, but show the ability to maintain ourselves by exhibiting self-control showing a pattern of temperance in all we do. Temperance involves self-control which is the ability to stay calm in difficult situations. I have known of people who appeared to be supper spiritual but lost the effectiveness of their witness due to a lack of self-control under pressure.

> *"I waited patiently for the LORD; and he inclined unto me, and heard my cry.*
> *He brought me up also out of an horrible pit, out of the miry clay, and set my feet upon a rock, and established my goings.*
> *And he hath put a new song in my mouth, even praise unto our God: many shall see it, and fear, and shall trust in the LORD."*
> *Psalms 40:1-3 KJV*

There are many blessings that await us as we walk into the divine will of God but one thing we must be willing to do, which actually is not a choice, if we are to receive anything from God, and that is to learn how to wait on God's will to be fulfilled in our lives. We cannot wait like a child who wants to go to the amusement park and keeps asking mom and dad are they ready to go yet? But we must patiently wait on the promises of God.

When we refer to God's increase it does not always suggest God will open the window and pour out natural blessings on us, but it does imply to us there will be many spiritual blessings that will come to us as we strive to live Godly in the sight of God.

Godliness has been defined as the quality of being devoutly religious, displaying piety or a man or woman of a God-like character. Whatever we do we should keep in mind that we are to reflect a spirit and a presence of God in our lives as we interact and communicate with others.

> *"Let your light so shine before men, that they may see your good works, and glorify your Father which is in heaven."*
> *Matthew 5:16 KJV*

> *"And to godliness brotherly kindness; and to brotherly kindness charity."*
> *2 Peter 1:7 KJV*

A life of godliness is reflected in the way we treat others. We cannot be selfish toward others and expect God to shower his blessing on our lives. We must have a love for one another that is pure and unselfish.

When we think of kindness and charity, we must also consider the word benevolent which implies a spirit of unselfish giving to others in need. If we are to be able to do for others with the right spirit we must develop a godly love for everyone even those who may not feel the same way for us.

> *"A new commandment I give unto you, That ye love one another; as I have loved you, that ye also love one another.*
> *By this shall all men know that ye are my disciples, if ye have love one to another."*
> *John 13:34-35 KJV*

Throughout this book we have focus on the fact that God does not want us to live a life void of his blessing but wants us to experience an increase in every area of our life. What is important for us to know is not only does God allows you and I to be recipients of his great treasures of blessings, but that God can trust us to magnify him with the increase he allows us to receive.

The God of Increase

> *"Pure and undefiled religion before God and the Father is this: to visit orphans and widows in their trouble, and to keep oneself unspotted from the world."*
>
> James 1:27 KJV

It is important to realize God not only blesses us with many increased blessings to show his love for us, but he also blesses us with tremendous increases to allow you and I to be a conduit by which he can use us to be a blessing to others.

The God of Increase

What areas in your life would you like to receive an increase? As you list the areas of your life that you would like to receive an increase in, I am praying with you and touching in agreement that you will receive, going forward, your greatest blessings ever.

_____
_____
_____
_____
_____
_____
_____
_____
_____
_____
_____
_____
_____
_____
_____
_____
_____
_____
_____

The God of Increase

How do you desire to be used of God as you receive your increase?

The God of Increase

What can or are you willing to do to receive your increase?

STEPS TO TAPPING INTO GOD'S HIDDEN TREASURES

- Develop a constant and strong Prayer life.
- Be diligent in the study of God's Word
- Build up your Faith in God
- Operate in Faith
- Be a doer of the word of God.
- Cherish God's word!
- Maintain fellowship with positive believers!
- Be a light unto others.
- Be a worshiper.
- Have a heart of thanksgiving.
- Be a blessing to others whenever possible.
- Expect to see God manifested in your life.

FAITH QUIZ

Do you believe in the power of God? ❏ Yes ❏ No

Do you believe in God? ❏ Yes ❏ No

Do you believe in prayer? ❏ Yes ❏ No

How often do you pray per week?
  (Circle one) 1 2 3 4 5 6 7 8 9 10 or more

Do you feel it is important to attend a house of worship? ❏ Yes ❏ No

How often do you attend worship services per month?
  (Circle one) 1 2 3 4 5 6 7 8 9 10 or more

How often do you read your per week?
  (Circle one) 1 2 3 4 5 6 7 8 9 10 more?

Do you see yourself as: ❏ Spiritual ❏ Religious ❏ Both

Do you believe in Miracles? ❏ Yes ❏ No

Do you share your faith with others? ❏ Yes ❏ No

Faith Quiz Additional Responses

In what areas can I make improvements in building my Faith?

As I walk into my blessing of increase how can I bless others?

THE GOD OF INCREASE

By faith what areas are you seeking God for an increase?

After reading through this book note the areas where you have experienced increases in your life

NOTES

The God of Increase

"Therefore, I say unto you, What things soever ye desire, when ye pray, believe that ye receive them, and ye shall have them."

Mark 11:24-26 KJV

As we continue to believe, asking our heavenly father for anything in prayer and faith, without doubting, we can look to God with expectation for abundance out of His vast hidden treasures.

Prepare to receive your blessings from God.

God's best for you is yet to come!

Dr. Anthony Walton, Author

www.ingramcontent.com/pod-product-compliance
Lightning Source LLC
Chambersburg PA
CBHW061944220426
43662CB00012B/2015